MOOF

MEMUKIES

True Tales From The North York Moors.

WRITTEN BY
KEITH SNOWDEN

CASTLEDEN PUBLICATIONS

PICKERING

ISBN 0 9514657 8 3

First published 1995
Reprinted 1997
Reprinted 1998
Reprinted 2000.

Typeset, Printed and Bound
at the press of the publisher
CASTLEDEN PUBLICATIONS
11,Castlegate, Pickering,
North Yorkshire, YO18 7AX
Telephone 01751 476227.

CONTENTS

INTRODUCTION

WHEN in 1956 I took over a moorland area as part of my insurance agency I was met with the greatest kindness and hospitality, being quickly accepted as a friend by my policyholders. I soon grew to love the people of the moors and to meet the many interesting personalities among them. I found the moorlanders to be amongst the most hard-working people I have ever met; able to endure many hardships which would finish many a townsman off.

Not all the memories in this book are mine, in fact very few of them, for some of the stories are beyond living memory, having been passed down through the generations, so it is well to keep them documented.

I possess a good memory for conversations and anecdotes, so where these recollections are on a personal basis, I have been able to record accurately.

Keith Snowden,
Pickering, 1995.

ACKNOWLEDGEMENTS

THE AUTHOR wishes to thank the following for their help and co-operation during the researching of this book:

Mrs Elfreda Aldridge, Mrs Elvie Bolderstone, Mrs Nancy Baxter, Mrs Nora Carter, Rev.T.H.Hicks, Mrs Florence Mackley, Dick Nichols Esq, Mrs Beatrice Pacitto, E.Winston Peel Esq, Mrs Mabel Simpson, John T.Peirson-Smith Esq, Rev.Arnold Pendlebury, Mrs Patricia J Sellars, Cecil Snowden Esq, Sid Spencer Esq, Peter N.Walker Esq, John Wilkins Esq, Mrs Ivy F.Woodward, Malton Library and the librarian, *Mercury* office, Scarborough.

Photographs are by the author, with the exception of those on page 37, Rev.Couse; Page 46, Peter N.Walker; and those on Page 15, which are over one hundred years old.

AT SALTERSGATE

JUST BELOW the bend known as *The Devil's Elbow* on the A169 between Pickering and Whitby stands the *Saltersgate Inn*. The original inn was built around 1630 of Flemish bricks. Formerly known as *The Coach and Horses,* it was as the name suggests, a coaching inn and when Charles Thistle took it over in 1929 the stables for horses, where a change was kept, were still in existence as were the Postboys beds in the attic.

In the days of the Salt Tax fish was smuggled from Robin Hood's Bay to be salted and the Thistles discovered that the salt cupboards were still in the kitchen and there were racks in the cellars where the fish would be dried. The Thistles had the place until 1960.

Early this century Major Mitchelson, of Pickering, arranged a shoot on the moors and it was made known to Mrs Hoggard, who was the landlady at that time, that King Edward was coming to lunch. Great effort was expended over several days to get everything shipshape and ready. On the morning of the appointed day there was a knock on the front door. When Mrs Hoggard opened it, two gentlemen standing there asked if they could have a glass of ale. The landlady said, 'Come your ways in and sit by the fire; you can have some ale, but you will have to drink it from a cup, 'cause t' king's coming.' The gentlemen were Major Mitchelson and the king. Just the sort of prank that the major would play on the landlady, for he was a great practical joker, and I'm sure the king would enjoy the caper also.

Mention of the fireplace reminds me that the inn is haunted by the ghost of a man who was buried under the fireplace. I once read a short story by a parson who told of a traveller who stayed the night at an inn and was murdered by the landlord for his money. He was buried beneath the fireplace and a legend was placed on the mantlepiece that as long as the fire burned, the house would stand. My old friend the late Mrs Johnson of Lockton told me she had known the parson, who used to spend his holidays in the area, so he must have got the idea for his story from the *Saltersgate Inn*, where the fire is supposedly never allowed to go out. The old turf fireplaces had a deep hole underneath to collect the ashes, which were like a fine silver sand. Mrs Johnson had such a fireplace and when Charles Laughton, the famous film star, made one of his frequent visits to Lockton, he found Mrs Johnson cleaning her fireside and he wanted to look down the hole. I think he must have read the same story as me.

Just accross from the inn was a shepherd's house, George Mackley, to whom I sold an insurance policy when he was sixtyfive and which he paid until he was eighty, and he was always a joy to talk to if I could catch him at home. In his latter days he developed a bad foot and to protect it from the wet and dirt of winter, he wrapped his foot in a large piece of oilcloth. I asked him if he had put anything on it. 'Aye,' he replied, 'Stockholm Tar', it cures sheeps feet, so it should cure mine.' I believe it did cure him. They gave him a party at the inn on his eightieth birthday and he gave me a glass of champagne which had been left over from the party, when I went to pay him out. It was the last time I saw him.

In 1962 there was a great fall of snow which blocked the road from Lockton. Florence Mackley and her husband had a narrow escape. They had moved from *Low Horcum*, a farmhouse in the bottom of the *Hole of Horcum,* to another farm because of a family dispute. Her husband came in just after the removal and said 'Horcum's down!' Florence couldn't believe it, but it was so. Some said it was an avalanche or a giant snowball which had rolled down the hill. Florence didn't believe that for there was no great heaps of snow near the ruins, but she thinks it was providential.

The Laughtons owned *Cherry Tree Farm* in the moorland village of Lockton, and when Frank was recovering from a serious illness he came to live there. It was decided to build a conservatory for him to convaless in and Charles specified that the base should be built of stone to match the house. After the work had started he paid a visit one weekend and found that the builders were using bricks. He kicked the lot down and they did use stone after that. On another occasion Charles had come to Lockton from Scarborough in his brother Tom's new car. Tom must have been 'showing off', for when it was time to go, Charles was missing. Eventually he was found wandering in the grounds, but announced, 'If Tom wants to break his bloody neck, he can, but I'm walking back!' And walk back he did, accross the moors.

One day Frank came on a motor-cycle combination with Charles as his passenger in the sidecar. When it was time to return to Scarborough it had started to rain. Charles refused to wear his new hat, preferring to shelter it in the sidecar, even if his head did get wet.

Mrs Sedman, who had the shop, was a big 'chapel body' and would not sell on a Sunday. Charles Laughton used to go and plead with her to sell him a quarter of chocolate toffees. She refused, of course,in spite of all his efforts. On one Sunday he said to Mrs Johnson, 'Well, I'll just go up and plauge [tease]Mrs Sedman.' 'I'm afraid, Mr Charles, you'll have to go the other way.' said Mrs Johnson. 'Why, what do you mean?' enquired the great actor. 'To the cemetery, she is dead.' was the reply, and Charles wept.

In his film, *Vessel of Wrath,* Charles Laughton in his character, Ginger Ted, having gained respectability by marrying a missionary, retires to a pub called *The Fox and Rabbit.*

During the Second World War a Home Guard unit

was formed in the Lockton area. The men were better off than the Pickering contingent, who only had one real gun and had to drill with wooden dummy rifles, for the moorland men were mostly farmers and they all had shotguns. The commanding officer was Mr Yarburgh Lloyd-Greame, of *Kingthorpe House.* Ralph Stothard, who had the garage at Lockton, told me the story of their first practice shoot which was held on Mr Lloyd-Greame's land. "Lloydie", as he was called behind his back, arrived in his car, which was specially made for him, as he had very long legs, the result being that nobody else could drive it as their feet would not reach the peddles. He had a flask of whisky in the car and kept going over to have a nip. The farmers brought their shotguns and Lloydie produced an Elephant gun, and, of course, he would have the first shot. A tree was chosen as the target and Lloydie let his gun off with a terrific report. 'What happened?' he asked. 'Nowt.' someone replied. He had another shot and a twig dropped out of the tree. 'Whaa! thoo can't shoot with that thing.'exclaimed one of the men. 'I'll have you know I've shot an elephant with this gun.' replied his C.O. 'Aye, it'd have to be a bloody elephant for thoo to see it!' said his critic.

As a young teenager I worked as a clerk for two brothers who were agricultural merchants and Mr Lloyd-Greame was one of our customers. He used to growl and grumble like an old bear when he came up the office stairs. He had been allocated three bags of seed wheat which, it being wartime, was expressly for the purpose of sowing. He gave two bags to his horse for feed and planted only one bag; the result being a very sparse growth for which he was fined. On his visit to the office just after the report was in the local paper, Mr Harold said, 'I see you've been in a bit of trouble, sir.' 'Yes,' he replied, 'I looked out of my window one day and I saw a man on MY LAND proding about with a little spade. I went out to him and said "You ought to have a little bucket to go with that".Ha, ha, ha; he didn't seem to like that.'

One day Lloydie noticed some workmen at the end of the lane. 'What are those men doing at the end of the lane, Parry?' he asked his gamekeeper. 'They're County Council workmen, sir, come to repair the road.' Mr Parry replied. 'Oh, good, as long as they are not too long about it.' said Lloydie. The folowing day they brought one of those green tent-like covers and set it at the side of the road as a shelter to have their lunch in, etc. 'Good God, Parry!' exclaimed Lloydie, 'The buggers must have come to stay, they've brought their bloody house with them.'

Later in my life I had to call on Miss Lawson, who was his faithful housekeeper – very faithful indeed, for she had a lot to put up with. He was now in his nineties and had been ordered to fell some trees by the roadside which were considered to be in a dangerous condition. Being an old autocrat, he hated to be ordered to do anything, so he did not comply with the instruction. The result was that he was summoned to the court at Pickering. 'Will he go?' I asked Miss Lawson. 'Well, he's getting ready to go and see his solicitor this morning.' she replied. Go he did and Brian Gardner, who was the Police inspector at the time, told me that Lloydie had a hot-water bottle at his back. Halfway through the proceedings the bottle had gone cold, so they had to fill it for him with more hot water. Mr Lloyd-Greame faded away following a stroke at the age of ninetyfour.

AT HUTTON-LE-HOLE

Hutton-le-Hole, Thou dear old spot,
Thou seems to say,'Forget me not';
I love the birds that all thee wing,
I love the heather and the ling.

(Emily Strickland.)

AT HUTTON-LE-HOLE there is a house with the inscription, 'By Hammer and Hand All Arts do Stand', which quotation is taken from the Blacksmith's Charter. The house was built by some ancestors of the present writer, Emmanuel and Betty Strickland, in 1784, as a beer house for their workers in an ironstone mine at Rosedale. We have to remember that tea was extremely expensive in those bygone days, and most ordinary people drank beer. Thomas Hardy, in his book *The Mayor Of Casterbridge* has his hero say:
'I don't drink it myself because of my oath, but I am obliged to brew it for my workpeople.'
So, the beer would be brewed on the premises. Apart from beer there was cider and porter.

In the directory of 1823 Robert Strickland is named as the blacksmith, and in White's directory for 1840 his address is given as the *Beer House*. It ceased to be a beer house in 1900.

The last of the Stricklands to own the house was John, who married Anne Poad, a member of a well-to-do Levisham family. John was a farm bailiff and unfortunately he lent a large sum of money to his employer. When that employer failed, the Strickland money was lost and John had to sell the house.

John and Anne had a daughter, Emily, who became an evangelistic preacher at the age of eighteen. When she preached in the Primitive Methodist chapel at Pickering, she filled the place to overflowing with a congregation anxious to see and hear this phenomenon. She made preaching tours travelling from place to place by pony and trap and being given hospitality by wealthy friends, just as Jesus Christ was. Her style of preaching must have been scathing; – they enjoyed a good haranguing sermon in those days, or so it would seem. An old lady in Wintringham told my stepfather that she remembered Emily preaching, and she said to them that 'The people of Wintringham put away their religion with their Sunday clothes!'

Emily developed a heart complaint and was advised by her doctor to change her lifestyle and give up preaching, but she said she would never do that. She was found dead in her cottage at Hutton, at the age of thirtysix, after she had been cleaning. in May 1901.

The owner of the house at the time of writing is Mr John Wilkins, who bought it in 1987, and runs it as a guest house. Unfortunately the deeds are incomplete, but it is known that a Mr John Winters lived there early this century; certainly during the 1914–18 war. He had made his money in Australia. The cottage to the north of the house was part of the outbuildings. Later it was a farm. A monk from Ampleforth owned it in the 1930s.

The house is haunted by a lady of about thirtyfive, who wears a long black dress.

The village was formerly known as Hutton i' the Hole; the Post Office added the 'le' with the Penny Post [1840] in Victorian times, as they did to many places to distinguish them from other places with such a name as Hutton, or Thornton. Other names attached to it appear as Hegehotun, and Hotununderheg. It has been estimated that that the place could date back to AD700, although the area was known to man before that time for flints of the Middle Bronze Age have been turned up by the plough. When the Danes invaded our area in AD876 they penetrated into many remote dales and some of the oldest settlements bear the names of Norse origin. Two farms near Hutton have such names, *Lund,* which is Old Norse for a small wood; and *Bainwood,*

13

Bain meaning Holly. After the Norman invasion the village was given to Stephen, a monk of Whitby Abbey, who started to build a monastery at Lastingham. Sometime before AD1087 the Norman lord of Kirkbymoorside added Hutton to the St.Mary's Endowment, so that the York abbey could claim to own all the land from the water of the Dove to the water of the Seven. Hutton became a part of the Manor of Spaunton, until the Dissolution of the Monasteries, when it was given to Lord Grey de Wilton. In 1566 the manor became a 'Freenhold Manor'.

Another interesting building in the village has the initials 'J.R.1695' and was formerly the home of a prominent Quaker, John Richardson. The carved initals, however,are those of his father-in-law, John Robinson. Mr Richardson travelled extensively and had many exciting adventures in America, where he became a friend of William Penn. John Richardson died at *Oxclose,* in 1754.

HAMMER & HAND, Hutton-le-Hole.

EMILY STRICKLAND, Youthful evangelist.

15

CROPTON LANE FARM, Scene of horrific murder.

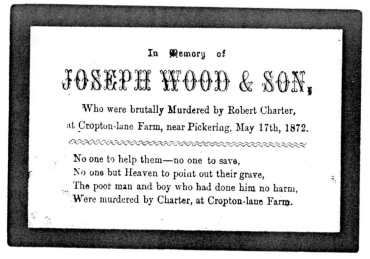

In Memory of

JOSEPH WOOD & SON,

Who were brutally Murdered by Robert Charter,
at Cropton-lane Farm, near Pickering, May 17th, 1872.

No one to help them—no one to save,
No one but Heaven to point out their grave,
The poor man and boy who had done him no harm,
Were murdered by Charter, at Cropton-lane Farm.

CONTEMPORARY MEMORIAL CARD.

16

MURDERS MOST FOUL

WHEN MY great-grandmother Frances Blakelock helped a feeble old man off the train onto the platform of Pickering Railway Station and was later told whom he was, she was horrified to realize that he was the killer in the case of the Cropton Lane Farm Murders.

It was in May 1872 that the disappearance of Joseph Wood, a respectable yeoman farmer of *Cropton Lane Farm*, aroused suspicions of the worst kind. They had last been seen on May 18th, and seemed to have vanished overnight. The boy, his eldest son, was about ten years old. Some days after this mysterious circumstance, a relative received a letter with a Liverpool postmark, purporting to be from Joseph Wood, saying that he was 'going foreign' for his health. The relative thought that there was something suspicious about this and called on the police. Details of Mr Wood's appearance were circulated to the ports and captains of the ships, but no one could throw any light on the matter. Another letter from Joseph Wood had been previously written to Mr Wood's brother inviting him to the funeral of a niece. The letters were compared and it was noted that the handwriting varied considerably between the two communications. It was concluded that the Liverpool letter was a forgery.

Nothing further was heard until November 7th, when one of the Woods was removing some straw at *Cropton Lane Farm* and a pair of boots were found in the straw house. The brother made a search of the house and in a cubby-hole under the stairs he found another pair of boots. Joseph was known to have only two pairs of boots and enquiries of his bootmaker revealed that he had not recently bought any more. Foul play was now definitely suspected and the brother decided to drag the pond. This operation revealed a coat; trousers with a quantity of silver and copper in the pockets; a shirt; waistcoat; and a knife which had belonged to the young boy. Police Superintendant John Jonas, at Pickering was informed and a start was made to drain the pond. Part of a human hand was found and it was examined by Dr John H.Walker of Pickering, who said it was the left hand of a grown human, cut off at the wrist and the fingers taken off.

Superintendant Jonas began a more thorough search of the farm buildings and the yard. The other hand and two feet were found buried near a stick-heap. The pile of sticks was removed and there were indications underneath that the ground had recently been dug up. A pair of trousers was found, but the hole had been large enough to hold a body, so it appeared that the body had been removed to another location.

There was no money found in the house, although it was believed that Mr Wood usually kept a considerable sum around.

In the meantime, Robert Charter of Lastingham, who was a cousin of Joseph Wood, was approached. It seems that the property occupied by Charter belonged to Joseph Wood, who was seeking repossession of it. Charter was asked if he had heard anything of Mr Wood and he produced a letter purporting to be from Liverpool. Enquiries revealed that on September 17th, Charter had called at Mr R.B.Wood's drapers shop in Malton and Mr Wood asked if there was any further news of his brother. Charter replied, 'No, but I wished he would come back as I would like to go back to my own house.

The body was found in a sack with a rope round the neck. The rope was slack, but there was also a black silk handkerchief which was tightly tied. Some bones were also found. One can imagine the sensation this case caused in a small town like Pickering, and when the inquest was held at *The Horse Shoe,* there was a very large crowd outside. The members of the Coroner's jury were asked to view the body, which was in an outbuilding at the rear of the Police House in Hallgarth. Some indications of the state of mutilation can be gathered from the fact that Joseph Wood's brother could only identify him by his whiskers, which resembled his own in style.

A brother of Joseph Wood had gone to Charter's house where some writing paper was found and when compared to the letter from Liverpool it was found to be the same. Two watches were found in a drawer, one of which belonged to Joseph Wood and the other to his father. Charter was charged with the murder of Joseph Wood, but denied it, saying, 'It was a pity I went to the house that night.' However, while Superintendant Jonas was away from home, Charter called at the Police Station and told the sergeant that he wished to make a confession.

Although a shirt had been found which had belonged to the boy there were no clues as to the whereabouts of his remains at this stage. When Charter was questioned about it, he said the boy had been devoured by the pigs. The following Sunday a large party of volunteers was assembled to scour the land at *Cropton Lane Farm*. Human bones were found among some spread manure on one of the fields and they showed signs of having been knawed by an animal. From signs in the boiler-house, it appeared that the poor boy's body had been first boiled and then fed to the pigs!

A two-day trial was held at York Castle in March 1873, and the jury, most amazingly, gave Charter the benefit of the doubt, finding him not guilty of murder, but guilty of maslaughter. He was sentenced to twenty years imprisonment.

Thirteen years after Charter had committed these terrible deeds, the house at Lastingham which had been occupied by him was demolished to make way for the *Darley Memorial School*. *The Malton Messenger* of May 2nd 1885, reported: The buildings and orchard belonged to and were occupied by Robert Charter, who was apprehended at this place by Supt.Jonas, of Pickering, for the murder of Joseph Wood, of Cropton, on the 17th May 1872.

It will be the recollection of many that the body of the murdered man had been dragged about after much mutilation, and that the greater part of it was in a sack secreted beneath the soil of an old water course in a field near Lastingham.

It will also be remembered that a child disappeared from the house of the murdered man on the night of the terrible transaction, and although the horrible hypothesis was set up at the time of the trial that the poor lad's body had been thrown to the pigs, still there was no satisfactory evidence on this point and from the time of those horrible and exciting scenes to the present, not the slightest clue to the poor missing child has ever been obtained.

Many of the villagers who volunteered to demolish the house expected to find human bones during the course of the work. Upwards of forty stalwarts with suitable tools assembled on Saturday morning. During the day ample refreshments in the shape of beef sand-wiches, tea and beer, were liberally carried round the volunteer workmen.

On Monday Mr Robinson Wood, of Aiskew House, had the honour of bringing in the first load of materials for the new buildings, and other teams included those of the late Mr Geo. Strickland, of Manor House, and Mr John Flintoft, both of Spaunton. These and others presented a gay appearance, as the horses had ribbons attached to them as if it were a gala

There is a ghostly footnote to the case, for it was said of *Cropton Lane Farm* that the blinds would not stay down over the windows.

No one pities Old Bob Charter
For the deed that he has done,
For he killed the poor old farmer
And his helpless little son.

Anon

20

Another murder case which set the Helmsley area agog was the one known as 'The Roper Moor Murder'. In 1894, Robert Heseltine Hudson, his wife and infant daughter arrived in Helmsley and took lodgings for a fortnight with a Mrs Holmes, in Bondgate. Hudson was a native of the district and he said he wanted to show his wife some of the scenes of his youthful days. He hired a pony and trap and took them out each day. Mrs Holmes said later that they appeared to be on friendly enough terms, but Mrs Hudson had remarked that he took her to such lonely places.

On Saturday June 8th, Hudson took his wife and daughter for another drive, setting off at eight in the morning. He returned alone at two in the afternoon and said that he had driven to his aunt's at Hovingham and that they had decided to spend the weekend there. Mrs Holmes told him he would need to take the child's clothes with him if they were staying. After he was gone, Mrs Holmes went into the bedroom which the Hudson's had occupied and found that the child's clothing was still there, but Mrs Hudson's clothes had been scattered about the room. Before leaving Hudson had said to Mrs Holmes that he was going to Birmingham for a week and that he and his wife would return on the following Monday.

On the Tuesday, Mrs Holmes received a letter in the name of Mrs Hudson, asking her to send her things to Darlington, as something had prevented her return to Helmsley. The letter was written in pencil.

Mrs Holmes had an unexpected visitor on the Friday night, for Mrs Hudson's sister from Sheffield arrived and brought with her a letter from Robert Hudson, which was written in pencil. A comparison was made with the previous pencil-written letter which was purported to have been written by Mrs Hudson, and the handwriting proved to be the same. Inquiries were made at the aunt's in Hovingham. She said she had expected them, but they had never arrived. By now tongues began to wag and the worst was begun to be suspected. It was noted that Hudson had bought a new spade at Trenan's ironmongers shop during his stay in Helmsley. Inquiries were made at the home of Hudson's parents in Darlington and the clothes that Mrs Holmes had forwarded were found there.

A search of the moors was made; no easy task when one considers that area above Helmsley which would have to be covered. It was a roadman and a butcher who found an area of newly-dug ground under a clump of trees on Roper Moor. A preliminary investigation revealed a child's hand and the police were then called to the scene. When the excavation was carried out, the mother's body was found with the child under her legs. Both of the victims had their throats cut.

Hudson was brought before the court at King's Heath, Birmingham on the 20th June. He pleaded guilty to the wilful murder of his wife and child. Hudson seemed anxious to get the proceedings done with as quickly as possible, for when the police sergeant was giving formal evidence of the arrest and his identification, the prisoner interrupted him by saying, 'Oh! come on, I am Robert Heseltine Hudson, the man you want.'

He was sentenced to death and the execution was carried out at York Castle on August 13th.

22

SALTERSGATE INN, The fire burns on.

DANBY LODGE, Now the Moors Centre.

23

DANBY CASTLE, Royal connections.

STORMY HALL, King Henry VIII legend.

24

A QUEEN IN ESKDALE

IT WAS to the north that Bluff King Hal, as Henry VIII was known, looked for his sixth, and as it turned out, his last wife, Katharine Parr. She was born at *Kendal Castle*, Westmoreland, in 1512. Her father was Sir Thomas Parr, a courtier, friend and boon companion to the king and he rose to be Controller of the King's Household. Her mother was a Lady-in-waiting to King Henry's first wife, Catherine of Aragon. The Parrs had a quarter share in the barony of Kendal and through her parents Katharine was descended from some of the greatest families in the north of England, including the Nevilles, by which connection she was related to the king.

When Katharine was five her father suddenly died, leaving her mother to bring up their three children. Resisting all proposals of marriage, Lady Parr devoted her spare time to the education of her children. Katharine also attended the royal school where she studied the humanities.

In 1521, Lady Parr negotiated with Lord Scrope of Masham for a marriage between Katharine and Scrope's grandson, a boy of fourteen. Agreement could not be reached on the financial terms, so the arrangements fell through. Her father had stipulated in his will that Katharine should marry a peer, or the son of a peer. There was not a great deal of choice for there was only some forty peers in the land, and most of these were already married. In 1525, at the age of thirteen, Katharine was married to the aged Lord Borough, who had a grown-up family from his first marriage to Anne Cobham. Lord Borough died some three years later, leaving Katharine a 'King's Widow', which meant that she was under the protection of the king and could not marry again without his consent.

For her second husband Katharine married John Neville, Lord Latimer of Snape and Danby, in 1533.

Lord Latimer was forty years of age and twice widowed, having a son and daughter, still children. He was a member of the House of Lords and a Gentleman Pensioner, one of that august band who formed the king's personal bodyguard. As well as the Snape and Danby estates, Lord Latimer had properties in Ryedale, including one of the three baronies at Thornon Dale, and at Sinnington. As Lady Latimer, Katharine and her husband would travel about their properties, when not having to attend matters of state in London.

Towards the end of Lord Latimer's life Katharine had met Thomas Seymour, a most romantic figure, and fallen in love with him. They planned to marry after the death of Latimer, but it was not to be, for King Henry shocked her by proposing to her after Lord Latimer's death in London in 1543. She could not refuse, but made the king wait for a period of mourning of six months.

There is rather a nice little romantic story with regard to this six month period. This concerns the farmhouse called *Stormy Hall,* which is said to have derived its name from a legend that King Henry VIII sought refuge here in a great storm one night, when on his way to visit Lady Latimer at *Danby Castle.* The story cannot be true, however, for King Henry is known never to have travelled further north than York.

Lord Latimer left only the one son, John, who had four daughters when he died in 1577. All married into great families: Katherine was married to the 8th Earl Percy of Northumberland; Dorothy married Burghley, Earl of Exeter; Lucy married Sir Wiliam Cornwallis; and Elizabeth married Sir John Danvers. Through this last marriage the Danby estate passed to the Danvers family and Sir Henry Danvers was created Earl of Danby. He sold it off in parcels to five freeholders of Danby, who, in 1656, sold it out again to various purchasers. The manor and several farms were bought by Sir John Dawnay of Cowick, an ancestor of the present Viscount Downe, for a sum of £4.10s2d.

Another Sir John Dawnay, a still earlier ancestor, married Dorothy, daughter of Richard Neville, Lord Latimer, the father of Katharine Parr's husband.

Danby Lodge, now the *North York Moors Centre,* was built by the Downes as a residence during the shooting season. It has been added to at different times.

Danby Castle is said to have been built in the early 15th century. The original fortress erected by Robert de Brus, a relation of the Scottish royal Bruces, is supposed to have stood at Castleton, and there is an old legend that the original castle was destroyed by fire, and that much of the stone was recycled and used in the present castle. The heraldry on the wall are those of the Roos and Latymer families. A Court Leet, the old baronial court, is still held at *Danby Castle.*

The castle bridge, sometimes known as *Duck Bridge,* after a stone mason called George Duck, who repaired it in the 18th century, bears the arms of the Neville family, and is of medieval design.

PUBS AND PARSONS

ACCORDING TO a tract published at York in 1806, the curate-in-charge's wife kept a pub at Lastingham. The pub could have been *The Blacksmith's Arms*. It may seem strange that a parson's wife should keep a pub, and yet we must remember that our Lord was born in the stable of an inn,and that his first miracle was to turn water into wine. Also were not inns attached to many a church in days gone by? Anyway, let me quote from the booklet:

The Rev.Mr.Carter, when curate of Lastingham had a very large family, with only a small income to support them, and therefore often had recourse to many innocent alternatives to augment it; and as the best of men have their enemies -- too often more than the worst, he was represented to the Archdeacon by an invidious neighbour, as a very disorderly character, particularly by keeping a public house, with the consequences resulting from it. The Archdeacon was a very humane, good man who had imbibed the principles, not only of a parson, but of a Divine, and therefore treated such calumniating insinuations against his subordinate brethren, with that contempt which would ultimately accrue to the satisfaction and advantage to such as listen to a set of sycophantic tattlers .... therefore at the ensuing visitation, when the business of the day was over, he in a very delicate and candid manner, interrogated Mr.C. as to his means of supporting so numerous a family......which was answered as related to me by one well acquainted with the parties, in the following words:-

"I have a wife and thirteen children, and with a stipend of £20 per annum, increased only by a few trifling surplice fees I will not impose upon your understanding by attempting to advance any argument to show the impossibility of us all being supported from my church preferment: But I am fortunate enough to live in a neighbourhood where there are many rivulets which abound with fish, and being particularly partial to angling, I am frequently so successful as to catch more than my family can consume while good of which I make presents to the neighbouring gentry, all of whom are so generously grateful as to requite me with something else of seldom less value than two or threefold. - This is not all: my wife keeps a Public-House, and as my parish is so wide that some of my parishioners have to come from ten to fifteen miles to church, you will readily allow that some refreshment before they return must occasionally be necessary, and where can they have it more properly than where their journey is half performed? Now, sir, from your general knowledge of the world, I make no doubt but you are well assured that the most general topicks, in conversation at Public-Houses, are Politics and Religion, with which, God knows, ninety-nine out of one hundred of those who participate in the general clamour are totally unacquainted; and that perpetually ringing in the ears of a Pastor, who has the welfare and happiness of his flock at heart, must be no small mortification. To divert their attention from these foibles over their cups, I take down my violin and play them a few tunes, no more liquor than necessary for refreshment; and if the young people propose a dance I seldom answer in the negative; nevertheless when I announce it time for their return they are ever ready to obey my commands, and generally with the donation of sixpence, they shake hands with my children, and bid God Bless them. - Thus my parishioners derive a triple advantage, being instructed, fed and amused at the same time: moreover, this method of spending their Sundays being so congenial with their inclinations, that they are imperceptibly led along the path of piety and morality.".....The Archdeacon very candidly acknowledged the propriety of Mr.C's arguments in defence of his conduct, and complimented him on his discernment in using the most convenient vehicle for instruction.

At Lockton there was a pub called *The Durham Ox.* Early this century the Church authorities bought it and closed it down, leaving the villagers the choice of *The Fox and Rabbitt,* or *The Horse Shoe* at Levisham. As a Scottish landlord once told me, when I remarked on the law at that time which allowed them to serve only travellers on a Sunday, and I said it must affect the trade in winter, 'Oh! I don't know,'he said, 'It is amazing what lengths people will go to for a drink.'

In 1946, the Rev. James Alfred Couse was appointed as Rector for the Lockton with Levisham parish and came to live at the Rectory. Known as 'Father Couse',(an Anglican Father) he was, I believe, a remarkable parson. While I was still a schoolboy attending the Church of England Day School in Hallgarth, Pickering, Mr Couse came as curate to the parish. He was young and attractive with an excellent singing voice, having been a noted chorister at Helmsley. He quickly caught the admiration of the young people and was responsible for more than one local lad entering the church. What drew me to him at that time was his use of visual aids. One Lent season he did a series of magic lantern lectures in the church, on *The Pilgrim's Progress.* I attended them all.

The Rev.Couse was born at Kirklington, near Thirsk, but spent part of his youth in Farndale, where his father was the police constable. He was educated at Queen's College, Birmingham, and his first curacy was at Easington, Spurn Point. The war interrupted his curacy at Pickering and he became a Padre to the A.R.P. He then became vicar of Paull, near Hull.

It must have been around that time that he met the Rev.Brian Hessian, Vicar of Aylesbury, Buckingham- shire. Brian Hessian was a great believer in visual presentation and at twentyseven was the youngest vicar in England. He sailed steerage to America where he found the negative of a silent film, *From The Manger To The Cross,* which had been made on the actual locations which Jesus Christ had trod. He brought it back and recorded a commentary, music and effects, at a cost of £5,000, of which he raised £2,000 on his securities and by mortgaging his home. The film packed *The Royal Albert Hall* three times daily for three months. Hessian formed the Dawn Trust and Bible Films Ltd, and bought further films from Hollywood.

It was one of these films that I noticed Father Couse

was to show at a Film Service in Lockton church. I said to my grandmother, 'Mr Couse is having a film service tonight and I am going, would you like to come along.' She said she would indeed. We were met at the door by the Rector, who gave us a royal welcome, 'Come in, my lord,' he said. It was a good turn out, for the villagers filled the church. I remember the first hymn was *O for a heart to praise my God,* and he sang his heart out that night.

Our friendship was based on films; I made some films for him when he was closely involved with religious duties, and I lent him some entertainment films for a Christmas Party when some films he was hiring did not arrive on time. I used to take him to the 'Ten Best Amateur Films', when they were shown, usually at York. One night we were going to a film show at Whitby and I had another friend with me. When we got to Ellerbeck, the Rector suddenly said, 'Of course you realize we're still in my parish. My friend looked out of the window and all that could be seen was the moor and a few sheep. 'But where are all your parishioners?' he asked.

Father Couse was not afraid of authority; as the Americans would say, 'He bucked authority.' He was not very enamoured of Donald Coggan when he became Archbishop of York, for he took all the Parish Registers to Bishopthorpe. 'He's pinched the parson's perks', he told me, 'If someone was tracing their ancestors and came to look at the registers, they paid a small sum, based upon the number of years one had to go back, and it was a little extra money for the parson.' Father Couse pointed out the poor salary a priest received, relevant to his education, but he said that was as it should be, for the Church should be a vocation, not a well-paid job.

Every day he walked up to the church at noon and rang the bell, a custom he valued to preserve. I remarked once that the authorities always seemed to send for him when some other vicar was in difficulties. 'Well, you see, I know all these little parishes.'he told me.

I met him towards the end of his life in Pickering and he said, 'We have a new Archdeacon at York and he sent for all the clergy's birth certificates; the idea being to give them the push when they reach a certain age. I didn't send mine, so this morning he sent me a postcard to remind me. I wrote on it "GO TO THE DIVIL" and sent it back to him'

Father Couse died in 1975 at the age of sixtyeight.

Eddie Sykes, a West Riding man who had been a ships cook, took over the *White Swan Hotel* at Newton-upon-Rawcliffe. He must have been fond of eating too, for at twentysix and a half stones he claimed to be the biggest landlord in the land. One evening, having concluded some business in the area, I decided to go into the *White Swan* and have a drink and see for myself this phenomenon. The only other man-mountain I had met in my life was Fred Pickup, a Pickering butcher, who weighed twentysix stones when he died. Eddie was big alright, and a customer passed a remark on the smartness of the suit he was wearing. 'You wouldn't think I bought it ready-made, would you?' he said. 'Nay,' said the customer, 'how could you do that?' 'I had a traveller called one day,' Eddie replied, 'and he said "I've got just the suit that would fit you, Mr Sykes." Eddie told him not to talk so daft. "Alright, I bet you a pint it will fit, I'll bring it next time I'm round." 'Sure enough, it fit well enough, as you remarked, so he got his pint, and when I paid him for the suit, he told me how it came about. The traveller said, "We made it to measure, of course, for a man of your size, but before we could deliver it, he died!"

Eddie Sykes may have been the biggest pub landlord,

but he met another gargantuan one day, who called for a drink. 'They tell me you're a big man,' said the stranger, taking off his jacket. 'Would you like to try my jacket on?' Eddie obliged and the jacket hung on him.

After the winter of 1968-69, the Sykes' gave up the *White Swan*. A few years later I met Mrs Sykes in Pickering. She said,'It were that last winter that did me; when I opened the back door and the snow was up to the top of the door-hole, that were it!'

Our moors in winter can be every bit as dangerous as a mountain. If the wind is in the north-east, there is nothing to stop it coming straight from the North Pole. Drifting is the major problem, and at its worst no machine can cope with it. Sid and Jennie Spencer, who had the *White Swan* at Newton after the Sykes', suffered a couple of bad winters. On one occasion snow had drifted to the top of the gable-end; a height of some seventeen feet. The outside gents toilet, which had no roof, was blocked solid with snow.

In 1962, when Fylingdales Early Warning Station was newly-opened, there was a terrific snowfall. Although the latest equipment was used to try and keep the road open, it blew in faster than they could clear it, and a considerable number of people who worked at the station were marooned. A special train was run up the valley and those who were seeking relief had to make their way over the snowy wastes to the train.

I have heard of people being found frozen to death after losing their way in a 'white-out' blizzard.

SPECTRAL HOUNDS

MY UNCLE, the late Ted Snowden used to tell of an experience he had when he was a young teenager. He started work as a messenger, or telegraph boy, at eight shillings a week. There were no telephone lines to such outlying places as moorland farms at that time, so the telegram was used for urgent messages. The telegrams would be delivered by the messenger, riding a heavy peddle-cycle, sometimes in the dark with an old oil lamp for illumination. It was one such night when he had to deliver a telegram to an out-of-the-way moorland farm some six miles from Pickering. He reached the farm alright and delivered the telegram and set off back to the office. Entering a stretch of road which was bordered with hedges, he thought he heard the sound of feet padding after him and glancing over his shoulder he saw an enormous black beast resembling a dog, but five times larger. He had heard of the 'Barghest', or 'spectral hound', the monstrous goblin dog whose appearance was said to be a harbinger of death to the beholder, or one of his family; and my uncle became convinced that this creature was one such. For the next mile or so he peddled for all he was worth, but the creature kept pace with him about twelve yards in the rear. Luckily the going was all downhill and he covered another two miles by which time the moon was shining fully, and on looking round he could see no sign of the supposed phantom; just the bare expanse of moorland road shining white in the moonlight. But could it have slipped passed him and be waiting for him further on, he wondered, so he kept up his pace until he thankfully entered the lighted streets of the town.

His friends at the Post Office told him he had been frightened by his own shadow. To be sure there was no death in the family immediately afterwards and he never saw the dog again. He was certain that it was not his shadow, because although the lane twisted and turned continuously, the beast remained always behind him.

The spectral hound known as the Barghest, Padfoot, and Guytrash, is well documented in England and on the continent of Europe. It was a spirit that could take on an animal form, not always a dog, but a bear or sheep. Usually it was malevolent or a bad omen, as my uncle pointed out.

The Black Dog is a different matter, for it has been known to be protective to people. It would seem that witches were afraid of a black dog, as one of the stories related by the Rev.Christopher Atkinson shows. A party of Westerdale freeholders were out hunting, but they had not met with any success. They came accross old Nanny, a noted witch. They told her of their disappointment at not being able to find a hare. 'Oh,' she said, 'I can tell you where you can find a hare ligging [lying], and a grand one and all, she'll give you a grand course. Only, whatever ye deea, mind ye dinna slip a black dog at her! That would be a sair matter for ye all.'

They promised they would not send a black dog after the hare and proceeded to the location Nanny had told them of. The hare led them a chase over several miles in parts of Westerdale Moor, over the Ingleby boundary, circling back by Hob Hole, when quite by accident a black dog joined in the chase. No one knew where it was from, but it attacked the hare as it was trying to get through a hole in the garden wall of old Nanny's cottage, tearing a piece out of the hare's haunch. Next day, some of the hunting party went to Nanny's home and found her ill in bed. She said she had happened an accident and lamed herself. She was found to have marks on her rear resembling the teeth marks of a dog!

In the sorting room at the Post Office the talk among the postmen turned to ghostly matters. 'Squam', who dabbled a bit in spiritism, liked to recount the story of his father coming in one night as white as a sheet. His wife said, 'Whatever is the matter, you look as if you have seen a ghost?' 'I have seen a ghost', her trembling husband replied, 'I saw a headless woman!'

'Whaa!' said Old Codge, a grumpy old postie, 'Ah've been out all hours of the night and ah've nivver seen nowt worse than missen!'

'No, and thoo isn't likely too!' fired back Squam.

THE GOOD SHEPHERD.

THE parson was giving religious instruction to a class at Stape School. He took as his theme Jesus's references to 'The Good Shepherd'; a subject warm to the hearts of hill farmers. At the end of his discourse he said, 'Now then children, if you were a flock of sheep, what would I be?' expecting them to say "The shepherd." Instead a voice from the back of the class piped up, 'T'auld tup!'

LASTINGHAM, Where a parson fiddled.

Rev. J.A.COUSE.   *Photo*: *Masser, Malton.*

LEALHOLME. Home of a bard-preacher.

BEGGAR'S BRIDGE, Built by a frustrated lover.

38

A BARD OF THE MOORS

JOHN CASTILLO, known as The Bard of the Dales, was born at Rathfarnum, in Ireland, three miles from Dublin, about the year 1792, of poor but honest parents; baptised according to his father's request, a Roman Catholic. After being shipwrecked off the Isle of Man, he arrived in England in his third year of age, and was brought up in the Eskdale village of Lealholme Bridge.

His father died when he was about eleven or twelve and he was taken from school and turned out into the world. Getting a job as a servent to a gentleman from Lincolnshire, he 'fell into a life of vanity', frequenting public houses, where he composed and sang songs of a humorous or satirical nature. One night, after drinking a considerable quantity of brandy, and crossing a churchyard he fell accross a grave where he suffered a terrifying fanciful experience, and upon sobering up he vowed to change his life and returned to Lealholme.

When he was nine he was engaged by a farmer at the Martinmass Hirings, and he began to think seriously about his soul's salvation. The people he went to live with, for farm lads 'lived in' at that time, were very serious, rigid church people and he received no help from them. A neighbouring farmer took in Methodist preachers, who frequently held services in the house and young Castillo went to hear them preach as often as he could. During a Wesleyan Methodist service, the sensitive lad broke down in tears. He recalled later, 'While we were pleading to God for mercy, all in tears, a thought struck me that "This is not the place, up get ye, let us be going; away, away, to the Roman Catholic priest; if the Methodists catch thee, what will he say? perhaps inflict a curse on thee which nothing can remove."'

The following Sunday he rose early and went to the priest's house, He was reluctantly admitted, but received no comfort from that quarter. He began to attend Mass and started to read some books of devotion which the priest had given him. About that time he became apprenticed to a stonemason. Being upbraided by the priest for going to hear a Gospel preacher, Castillo became disillusioned with the Roman Catholics and started to go to meetings of various denominations, walking as far as ten miles to hear a Gospel sermon.

He joined a Wesleyan class in April 1818. After much soul-searching, eleven months later, in the little chapel at Danby End, he was convinced that Methodism was the means of his salvation. Some of the Roman Catholics attacked him, which caused him to compose a poem, *An Address To My Roman Brethren.*

Being born in Ireland, where there are no snakes, he found some fame for curing the bites and stings of venemous reptiles, which led him to experiment with these creatures. He used to catch them in summer, and take them about with him to his work, and amuse or frighten the company he fell into with their manoeuvers. At one time he had a very large reptile which he kept in a wired box, so that persons may see it without danger. When sporting with the hagworm one evening, and making it appear he could do anything with it, on a sudden it reared up and stuck one of it's fangs into his finger, which by morning was fearfully swollen. By medical advice and the aid of Mr Ripley of Whitby, it was cured.

John Castillo became a lay preacher and in February, 1838 he was preaching in the Pickering circuit. One of the ministers he mentions in his notes was the Rev. Joseph Kipling, whose son, John Lockwood Kipling, the father of Rudyard Kipling, had been born in Pickering the previous year.

Castillo died in Birdgate, Pickering in 1845 and was buried in the Methodist graveyard, behind the former

Wesleyan Chapel on Hungate. The graveyard has since been levelled and part of it used for the building of a new housing estate. At the time of writing, the headstone from his grave is preserved by Mr John Hill. On the headstone is a quotation from his poem, *Auld Isaac:*

Bud noo his een's geean dim i' deeath,
Nae mare a pilgrim here on eeath,
His sowl flits fra her shell beneath,
    Te reealms o' day,
Whoor carpin care an' pain an' deeath,
    Are deean awy.

and the inscription reads, 'He lived for others'.
Over one hundred of Castillo's poems have been published. Some writers have compared him to Robert Burns, the national poet of Scotland. There are some similarities in that both men were reared on the land and worked close to nature. Castillo had Burns' feeling for animals; he wrote a poem *To A Horse Dying Alone.* But their lifestyle was completely different, whereas Burns was a reprobate, there is no indication of sex or biting satire in the poems of the Yorkshire bard.

SOME STAPE WITCHES

There are more things in heaven and earth,
Horatio, Than are dreamt of in your
philosophy. *(Shakespeare: Hamlet)*

WERE WITCHES figments of the imagination of our forebears? Was it superstition that made them take various precautions against certain women who had the reputation of practicing the black arts? Scientists would have us believe that such was the case, but our ancestors acknowledged their dark powers. Many a cottage had a 'Witch Post' in the fireside, a post made of witch hazel, or rownantree, as a guard against witchcraft. Some women carried a piece of witchwood in their purse as an added protection, in case they met a witch on their travels. A visit to the Wise Man would be one means of breaking a curse. He would recommend some ritual; it may be rather grizzly, such as taking the heart out of a bewitched animal and sticking new pins, new needles and new nails in it, and in the dead-of-night burn it on a bed of red-hot rowan ashes whilst reciting two verses of a certain psalm.

Johnnie, a farmer now retired to Newton-upon-Rawcliffe, formerly resided at Stape. He is a descendant of generations of the same family who lived at the former farmhouse and well remembers his 'auld folks' talking about local witches. There was no doubt in their minds about the evil influence of these women, for there was more than one in the Stape and Newton area.

One women in particular had the evil reputation. Her name was Jaques and she lived at *Rawcliffe Farm,* Stape. This sorceress was credited with possessing the power to put evil spells on animals. If an animal fell unacountably ill, the farmers believed it had been bewitched by her. It would seem that Ms Jaques also had the ability to remove the spell at will; doubtless for some financial consideration, or payment in kind.

There was one particularly unfortunate family to whom

Ms Jaques gave special attention, 'plagueing' [annoying] them with her spells. The Hollidays occupied a neighbouring farm, known as *High House,* and on one occasion they had a sick cow, so went to seek the help of the witch.

'Well, lads,' she said, 'It's a pity about your cow, but we'll have a cup of tea and then perhaps the beast will rise again.'

Sure enough; after they had partaken of the refreshment and returned to the cowhouse, the animal was on it's feet and seemed perfectly well again. The Hollidays had no doubt that the spell had been cast by the witch in the first place.

On another day the Holliday lads were on the Stape road with their horse-drawn wagon, and as soon as the horses reached the gate leading to Jaques's house they stopped dead. No amount of coaxing could persuade them to move. One of the brothers got down to examine the brake-blocks to see if they were binding. Then they heard a voice say, 'I doubt you're fast lads!' It was then that they noticed the witch standing at her gate. By now the lad inspecting the brakes had his hand through the wheel spokes. Suddenly the horses started forward and the the poor lad's arm was broken.

Young Tommy Holliday had to call at Jaques's one evening on some errand; one can imagine with what fear and trepadition, but the crone chatted with him amiably enough on the doorstep. Tommy had been to market and was sporting his latest acquisition, a pair of brand-new corduroy breeches. Just as he was taking his leave of the hag, she said, 'That's a fine pair of new breeches you've got on, Tommy.'

'Yes,' replied the unsuspecting youth, 'I bought them in Pickering today.'

'You'll have to mind you dont fall and split the knees out of them!' warned the hag.

Tommy's way home was a short-cut accross several

fields. As he turned, after closing a gate, a great old hare shot accross his path and startled him, causing the hapless youth to fall and split both knees out of his brand-new breeches. The Hollidays believed that Jaques had turned herself into a hare to frighten Tommy into falling and thus fulfill the prediction contained within her warning.

Shape-shifting, or transmogrification, was commonly attributed to witches and most primitive people believed that human beings could change their shape, taking on the appearance of animals, fish, birds and reptiles. As a result of this grew the tales of were-wolves and the like. The hare was commonly associated with witches in North Yorkshire and some of these were recorded by the Rev.J.C.Atkinson in his book *Forty Years In a Moorland Parish,* which was published in 1892.

In 1823, a certain George Calvert made notes about *Witch Hags who have dwealt hereabouts.* In the Pickering area he noted Nancy Nares, 'who did use the evil eye, could turn herself into a cat, had a familiar, was well up in matters of the black art and did use a crystal.' Nanny Pearson of Goathland 'could cripple a quickening [new-born] bairn.'

Other witches who possessed some of the aforementioned abilities listed by Calvert, were Nan Skaife of Spaunton Moor, who was also known as Mary or Jenny. She had the reputation of being able to foretell future events. She had a formula for making a magic cube. These magic cubes were used for the telling of fortunes. Auld Mother Migg of Cropton, (her real name was Sabrina Moss) did use the crystal. Sally Craggs of Allerston also used the crystal and could turn herself into a cat. Dinah Suggit of Levisham could also turn herself into a cat. She also had a familiar. Hesther Mudd of Rosedale 'did use the evil eye' and Emma Todd of Ebberston was 'well up in matters of the black art.' 'All these,' wrote Calvert, 'were at one

RAWCLIFFE OLD HOUSE, Erstwhile home of a witch.

FAIRY CROSS PLAIN, Haunted by little beings.

45

GOATHLAND, Gem of the moors.

PETER N. WALKER

time of great note and did in their day work great deed and cast many an evil spell and charm and were held in fear by great many good and peaceful folk.'

It was believed that a witch could only be injured by a silver bullet. Johnnie recalled the story of a witch who lived in a cottage at the top of Newton-upon-Rawcliffe. The old hag, in the form of an hare, was prone to play tricks on a certain farmer who resided some little distance from Newton. This old crone wreaked havoc with his crops and caused him various forms of annoyances. He had taken great pains to make a beautiful haystack, all neatly rounded and finished off with a nicely shaped top. During the hours of darkness the old witch had been at work and next morning his beautiful haystack was no more; just a scattering of hay all over the stackyard. That did it! He somehow or other procured a silver bullet and watched for the appearance of the hare. When the creature ultimately came, the farmer let drive with his gun and the hare was wounded in the leg and limped away. Next day the old crone was visited in her cottage and was found to be ill in bed with a bad leg.

Canon Atkinson, in his *Glossary of the Cleveland Dialect,* mentions the 'Gabble Ratchet', a name for a yelping sound at night, like the cry of hounds, and, he says, probably due to flocks of wild geese flying by night, taken as an omen of approaching death. This reminds me that Johnnie's family heared a sound like a trumpet in the valley and saw something white flutter up. Next morning they heard of the death of a neighbour in the dale.

Are witches real or imagined? John Wesley wrote in his *Journal* May 25th, 1768, It is true likewise, that the English in general, and indeed most of the men of learning in Europe, have given up all accounts of witches and apparitions, as mere old wives fables. I am sorry for it; and I willingly take this opportunity of entering my solemn protest against this violent complement, which so many that believe the Bible pay to those who do not believe it. I owe them no such service. I take knowledge, these are at the bottom of the outcry which has been raised, and with such insolence spread through the nation, in direct opposition, not only to the Bible, but to the suffrage of the wisest and best of men, in all ages and nations. They well know (whether Christians know it or not) that the giving up of witchcraft is, in effect, giving up the Bible...'

According to an article in *The Guardian* newspaper of March 6th, 1985, witchcraft is booming. church-yards have been desecrated in dead-of-the-night raids and in some cases bodies dug up for use in the black arts. At a rough estimate it is believed that there are now something like 80,000 witches in Britain.

The Daily Mail on July 27th, 1989 reported a case of attempted murder in which the victim's wife had been associating with a man who studied witchcraft. This man wrote to the author of one of his black magic books, and for £25 obtained a Voodoo Doll of his victim which had to be stabbed and strangled! This case reminds me of a lady I knew, who, as she was getting elderly, took in a male partner to help run her business. On the face of it he was a charming and attractive young man, but she became more embroiled in his affairs, renting a property of hers to his mother. Things started to go wrong, the mother did not pay the rent and the property was badly treated, so she tried to get rid of them. On going into the flat above the shop one day, she was horrified to find a doll of herself with pins sticking in it.

I bought a second-hand book which the bookseller informed me he had obtained from a witch. I hasten to add that the book was nothing to do with witchcraft, but was concerned with mythical history.

The Ryedale Mercury of November 3rd, 1990 carried a front page story in which a woman said she had taken part in witchcraft rituals. According to her there are at least thirteen covens active between Scarborough and Helmsley. Her story gives accounts of ritual killings, naked sex initiations and Satanic chants, at secret gatherings in the woods and forests of the district. She claimed there are Satanists in Pickering, Kirkbymoorside, Helmsley and Scarborough, from all backgrounds, including many professional people. This lady, in her early forties, first went to an occult gathering with a friend 'for a laugh'. This was in a secret location in Dalby Forest and about fortyfive people took part. They seemed really normal, just standing around and chatting; then the leader arrived, and gradually they split into smaller groups, sitting, kneeling, and lying on the ground. They formed what she later realized was a pentagram and slowly the talk turned into chanting. There were thirteen people in each group-the number needed for a coven. This lady learnt that forest clearings were always used for big events, such as ritual sacrifices, where chickens were split with a knife, then the blood and innards were smeared on the faces and bodies of the coven members. Initiation ceremonies also took part in the woods; the novice being forced to stand naked, with the coven sitting in a circle outside, before having sex with one of the leaders.

Some gatherings were held in members houses, the carpet would be rolled back to reveal a pentagram painted on the floor. Their leader, or Chief Wizard, would call on the Prince of Darkness. The woman said many of the members believed they were 'White Witches', using their powers for good, and would be horrified to find that they were worshipping the Devil. However, she maintained the leaders and acolytes knew exactly what was going on, and she had no doubts after spending one Hallowe'en among the graves of a Pickering churchyard. They danced among the graves, and people made shapes of upside-down crosses in the ground. The leader called to the Prince of Darkness. He said, 'Your people are waiting for you.' The woman then saw a figure which she described as 'the horned god'. This experience so frightened her that she resolved to begin the slow process of breaking away from the cult. She issued the following warning to others who were involved. 'Get out quick. You think you are in control of the power, but you are being manipulated. You are in great danger!'

Witches, it seems, are still very much with us.

THE LOVER'S BRIDGE

THE STORY of the *Beggar's Bridge*, near Glaisdale, is well-known and has been told elsewhere. It was erected in 1611 by one Thomas Ferris. I came accross this old poem, written by 'a Lady':

> The dalesmen say that their light archway
> Is due to an Egton man,
> Whose love was tried by a whelming tide;
> I heard the tale in its native vale,
> And thus the story ran:-

"Why lingers my loved one? Oh! why does he roam
On the last winters evening that hails him at home?
He promised to see me once more ere he went,
But the last rays of gloaming all lonely I've spent -
The stones at the fording no longer I see -
Ah! the darkness of night has concealed them from me."

> The maiden of Glaisdale sat lonely at eve,
> And the cold stormy night saw her hopelessly grieve;
> But when she looked forth from her casement at home,
> The maiden of Glaisdale was truly forlorn!

For the stones were engulfed where she looked for them last,
By the deep swollen Esk, that rolled rapidly past,
And vainly she strove with her tear bedimmed eye
The pathway she gazed on last night to descry.

Her love had come to the brink of the tide,
And to stem its swift current had repeatedly tried.
But the rough whirling eddy still swept him ashore,
And relentlessly bade him attempt it no more.
Exhausted he climbed the steep side of the brae,
And looked up the dale ere he turned him away;
Ah! from her fair window a light flickered dim,
And he knew she was faithfully waiting for him.

THE LOVERS VOW.
"I go to seek my fortune, love,
In a far and distant land,

And without thy parting blessing, love
　　I'm forced to quit the strand.

But over Arncliffe's brow, my love,
　　I see thy twinkling light;
And when deep waters part us, love,
　　'Twill be my beacon bright.

If fortune ever favour me,
　　St.Hilda! hear my vow!
No lover again in my native plain,
　　Shall be as thwarted as I am now.

One day I'll come to claim my bride
　　As a worthy and wealthy man!
And my well-earned gold shall raise a bridge
　　Accross the torrents span."

"The rover came back from the far distant land,
And claimed of the maiden her long-promised hand;
But he built, ere he won her, the bridge of his vow,
And the lovers of Egton pass over it now."

IN THE GOODLAND

GOODLAND, GOADLAND, and GODELAND are all names that have been applied to Goathland. Godeland is a dependant manor of the ancient honour of Pickering forest, and has been, from an early period in the possession of the Duchy of Lancaster. In former times, the tenants were bound by the tenure of their lands, to protect the breed of a large species of hawk, that nested on *Killing Noble Scar,* for the king's hunting.

Before the Whitby to Pickering railway came, the village was isolated from the outside world, margined on either side by elevated moorland, on the steep side of which was a luxurious growth of woodland. From the numerous howes and tumuli scattered over the moors in the vicinity of Goathland, it is evident that man has lived here from the earliest times. King Henry I granted the Benedictines a cell here, where Osmond, a priest, with a few companions, took up his abode. Subsequently it became a dependent cell to the Abbey at Whitby, but was vacated before the Reformation. It was dedicated to the Blessed Virgin, and is supposed to have stood on the site occupied by a farmhouse known as *Abbot's House.*

Goathland has been chosen by film-makers for its scenic value and is now easily accessible, not being far from the main Whitby to Pickering road. It has been made well-known through the North York Moors Railway, which has brought the station back to life, and having been chosen as the location for the making of the televison series *Heartbeat,* based on stories by a local author; about whom, more later.

Goathland is also associated with old customs and for its company of Sword Dancers. Plough Monday is the first Monday after the twelfth day of Old Christmas. After a service in the church the men known as 'Plough Stots', would drag a plough round the village. Some of them, known as 'Madgy-Pegs', dressed up bizzarely, amusing the villagers with their antics and collecting money, perhaps for the purchase of new candles for the church. Woe betide anyone who would not contribute to the Madgy-Pegs, for they may have had a furrow ploughed accross their lawn, or the grass in front of their cottage. The Plough Stots then performed a play and sword dance, a ceremony, which it is thought may date back to the time when the Danes ruled this area.

A procession preceded the play in which between sixteen and forty males would take part; the party being headed by the 'King and Queen', or 'Gentleman and Lady'. They were followed by the 'Toms', who were dressed in an eccentric fashion, disguised with make-up and clowning about to entertain the spectators. The Madgy-Pegs, who were men dressed up as women, would go around rattling tins to collect money to pay for a feast and dance, usually held in the local pub and to which the lasses, who had made the ribbons and costumes, would be invited. Next came the Sword Dancers, arranged in sets of six, and the fiddler who played the music for the sword-dancing; then the Plough Stots, pulling a plough. Bringing up the rear were 't'auld man and 't'auld woman, Isaac and Betty.

The Plough Stots were controled by a teamster, who wore a short frock and applied a whip upon the heads and bodies of his team. A bladder was attached to the end of the whip cord and was filled with dried peas, causing a rattle when wielded. Before the play was commenced the following was sung:

'We're Goadlan' Pleaf Stots cum'd ageean;
An' deck'd wi' ribbons fair;
Seea noo we'all deea't best we can
An't best can deea neea' mare.'

[We are Goathland Plough Stots come again,
And decked with ribbons fair;
So now we'll all do the best we can,
And the best can do no more.]

The sword dancers arranged themselves in a ring with swords raised and performed several slow and simple movements. Gradually the movements became more complex and the pace quickened. At the end of the dance the swords were interlocked to form a pattern which took the form of a cross in the middle. This was done with such skill that one man would be able to hold it above his head without a sword falling out of place.

During the week the company would tour the villages, the final performance being given in Whitby on the Saturday night.

The full ceremonial, of which the above is a short description, was made moribund in the late 19th century. In 1923 the custom was revived, but on a more modest scale; it continues to the present day, consisting of sword dancing, usually to the delight of summer visitors at special functions. There is a 'Blessing of the Plough' service in the church on Plough Sunday.

Goathland has had its share of ghostly happenings, and the villagers took matters of the occult very seriously. They appointed a 'Watcher', who would stand where the Goathland and Beck Hole roads join. By staring hard towards the bottom of the dale he would forcast how long it would be before a death occurred. There is also a ghost story connected with the stream at *Water Arc Fall*. It was said to be a dead warrior who cried out from the pool below the fall. His spirit was laid to rest by a Scottish visitor, who played a lament on his bagpipes from the fall to the village church. A house which had belonged to a tailor at Green End was said to be haunted by his apprentice. It seems that the tailor and his wife were fond of cards and would invite people to Green End to play. The apprentice boy noticed that they won more often than not, so taking particular note, he observed that they were cheating. Unfortunately he was fool enough to mention this to them and he was never seen again in the flesh. George Calvert, who wrote some notes on witches in 1823, also wrote of one Roland Burdon, who possessed a 'Holy Seal': 'This same Roland did slay in single combat the great worm or dragon which at one time did infest Beck Hole to the loss of many young maidens the which it did at sundry times devour. He slew it after a fierce battle lasting over half a day through the power of the Holy Seal being about his person. This worm did also infest Sneaton Moor.'

Yorkshire Television chose Goathland as the 'Aidensfield' of the series of Constable books by Nicholas Rhea, a pseudonym for Peter N.Walker, who was a native of Glaisdale. Peter's mother's name was Rhea, and although he made a career in the police force, rising to the rank of inspector engaged on public relations, he was writing all his spare time. Under his pseudonym of Nicholas Rhea he took over the column formerly written by the late J.Fairfax-Blakeborough in the *Darlington and Stockton Times*. Under another pen-name, Christopher Coram, he has written a series of detective novels. Writing under his own name he has penned books on the North Yorkshire Moors. He now lives at Ampleforth.

Since the showing on television of the *Heartbeat* programme, [in its fourth series at the time of writing] tourists have flocked to Goathland, and other Production companies have used the village for location work.

IN THE ESK VALLEY

WHEN THE Rev.John Christopher Atkinson accepted the living of *St.Hilda's church* at Danby, with an annual income of £95, he found things in a rather dilapidated state.The year was 1847 and he was thirtythree years old. Atkinson was born at Goldhanger, in Essex, where his father was a curate. Going to school at Kelveden, he later entered St.John's College, Cambridge, as a sizar, eventually taking his degree; he was ordained in 1842.

His predecessor at Danby was Joseph Duck, but he had not, as Atkinson put it, 'been famed for strength of body nor energy of mind and purpose; so that while there were Wesleyan Methodists and Primitive Methodists, in numbers and organization alike considerable, churchmen were not conspicuous in either the one respect or the other; a condition of matters which of course need occasion no surprise under the circumstances.'

When the Rev.Duck took Atkinson to see the church, he did not bother to remove his hat upon entering the building. Later Atkinson found the clerk having a pipe of 'baccy in the sunny embrasure of the west window. This man was also the schoolmaster, despite his lack of education.

Christopher Atkinson soon began to be fascinated by the local people and to learn the dialect, a mixture of Danish and Saxon, which was no mean fete for a Southerner. He heard from one old woman on whom he called, that *Fairy Cross Plain* was haunted by fairies. The house of that name was formerly a public house and stood where two roads crossed. It was believed that the fairies lived underground, as when seen they disappeared into a culvert. Asked if she had seen them, she replied in the negative, but said she had heard them making butter at night and the next day found some of their butter smeared on the bars of a gate.

The Reverend was also told about the 'Hobs', little chaps with a lot of hair covering them. Similar beliefs are held in other parts of the world; the Norwegian 'Trol', or the Danish 'Nisse' spring to mind; such a one was Peer Gynt, immortalized in the music of Edvard Grieg, and Till Eulenspiegel, whose capers inspired Richard Strauss to write a suite. These Yorkshire Hobs were either helpful or mischievous. Christopher heard the story of the *Hart Hall* Hob, in Glaisdale. The little man used to work while the family were asleep, flailing the corn, or churning the butter. It was said that the Hob did not like to be seen, but curiosity got the better of one of the lads in the house and in the dead-of-night he sneaked downstairs and, unobserved by the little fellow, saw him working hard with the flail. The lad described the Hob as a little brown fellow, almost naked and covered in hair. The family felt sorry for the creature and decided to make a cloak to protect him from the cold of winter nights. They placed it where he would find it when he came again, but when he found it, he realized he had been seen and said he would come no more.

Another story of the *Hart Hall* Hob related by Rev. Atkinson concerns a wagon loaded with hay. It was catchy weather and the load had been hard won, and as it was being led towards the stackyard, one of the wheels fell into the rut between the two stones of a water course. Extra horses were brought to try and realease the vehicle, but all to no avail. After several attempts and the light beginning to fail, it was decided to tackle the job first thing next morning. During the night Hob had been at work and it says much for his strength that when the men went out at dawn, the cart was in the stackyard and the hay stacked in an exemplary fashion.

Chrsitopher Atkinson also heard of the Wise Man of Stokesley. The Wise Man of ancient folklore was regarded as a wizard and the chief of witches; and yet the foe of witches in that he could be applied to for the purpose of undoing a spell. John Wrightson, of Stokesley, was written about in *Brand's Popular Antiquitites,* the author purporting to be 'A Yorkshire Gentleman', who wrote in 1819 as follows:

Imoposters who feed and live on the supersticions of the lower orders are still to be found in Yorkshire. These are called Wise Men, and are believed to possess the most extraordinary powers in remedying all diseases incidental to the brute creation, as well as the human race; to discover lost or stolen property, and to foretell future events. One of these wretches was four years ago living at Stokesley in the North Riding of Yorkshire; his name was John Wrightson, and he called himself the seventh son of a seventh son, and expressed ostensibly the calling of a cow doctor [cow leech it should have been]. To this fellow people whose education, it might have been expected would have raised them above such weakness, flocked; many came to ascertain the thief, when they had lost any property; others for him to cure themselves or their cattle of some indescribable complaint. Another class visited him to know their future fortunes; and some to get him to save them from being balloted into the militia, – all of which he professed himself able to accomplish. All the diseases which he was sought to remedy he invariably imputed to witchcraft, and although he gave drugs which have been known to do good, yet he always enjoined some incantation to be observed, without which he had declared they could never be cured. This was sometimes the act of the most wanton barbarity, as that of roasting a game-cock alive, etc. The charges of this man were always extravagant; and such was the confidence in his skill and knowledge, that he had only to name any person as a witch, and the public indignation was sure to be directed against the poor unoffending creature for the remainder of her life.

William Henderson, writing in *Notes On The Folk Lore Of Northern Counties Of England And The Borders,* says: His private character appears to have been very bad: still, his influence in Stokesley was so great that he was constantly in request as godfather to the children of the place; and on these occasions he used to attend church in a scarlet coat, a long white waistcoat and full-starched shirt-frill, crimson knee-breeches, and white stockings...... Wrightson used always to say that he had no power or knowledge beyond other men except when fasting, that he owed his powers to his being the seventh son of a seventh daughter, and that he was quite unable to transmit them to his own son.

In 1808, Wrightson went to live in Malton, where he appears to have continued his practices. He was brought before the court and convicted, but on his way to prison he committed suicide.

In the course of his parochial duties the Rev.Atkinson would walk thirty or forty miles in a week. Towards the end of his life, he estimated that he had travelled at least 70,000 miles in performance of his duties, and more than 70,000 miles in pursuit of his hobbies. He was a keen archaeologist and local historian, excavating burial mounds and other sites. He had his own theories about certain matters, such as the so called early British settlements, which he maintained were nothing more than gravel pits. He wrote *A History of Cleveland, Glossary of the Cleveland Dialect, Memorial Of Old Whitby,* and his masterpiece, *Forty Years In A Moorland Parish;* as well as books for children, including, *Jack of Danby Dale.*

Canon Atkinson served the parish for fiftythree years, and died in 1900.

FINIS.

LOCAL & REGIONAL HISTORIES BY KEITH SNOWDEN

KINGS IN RYEDALE
Covers 2,000 years of Ryedales association with royalty.
A delightful volume of which he can be justifiably proud.
Nicholas Rhea, *Darlington & Stockton Times.*
AUTHOR'S FIRST EDITION. £1.95. Post 33p.

PICKERING THROUGH THE AGES, The Second Edition.
Now revised and enlarged, with extended text and
many more pictures. Tells the story of the town from its
foundation in pre-historic times to the present day.
£2.70. Post 44p. ISBN 0 9527548 2 7.

HELMSLEY & KIRKBY THROUGH THE AGES
Here is the story of these two ancient Yorkshire market
towns and the many famous people connected with
them.
£2.85. Post 44p. ISBN 0 9514657 4 0

MALTON & NORTON THROUGH THE AGES
The story of these ancient sister towns, their noble
owners and famous sons.
REVISED EDITION. £2.85. Post 44p. ISBN 0 9514657 3 2

THORNTON DALE THROUGH THE AGES
Here is the story of one of Yorkshires prettiest villages and
the famous people connected with it.
NEW EDITION £2.95. Post 44p. ISBN 0 9527548 6 X.

SCARBOROUGH THROUGH THE AGES
The story of the Queen of English Watering Places.
REVISED & ENLARGED EDITION.
£2.95. Post 44p. ISBN 0 9514657 9 1.

THE CIVIL WAR IN YORKSHIRE
An account of the battles and sieges and Yorkshires
involvement. One of our best-sellers.
£2.95. Post 44p. ISBN 0 9514657 6 7.

WHITBY THROUGH THE AGES.
Pages from the history of this ancient Yorkshire sea port.
AUTHOR'S EDITION. £2.95. Post 44p.
ISBN 0 9527548 5 1.

KATHARINE PARR OUR NORTHERN QUEEN
The life and Northern associations of the last wife of King Henry VIII. A unique biography.
£2.95. Post 44p. ISBN 0 9514657 7 5.

MOORLAND MEMORIES
True tales from the Whitby and Pickering Moors.
AUTHOR'S EDITION. £2.85. Post 44p.
ISBN 0 9514657 8 3.

GREAT BATTLES IN YORKSHIRE
Recounting the many battles on Yorkshire soil from the Romans to the Roundheads.
NOW REPRINTED. £2.95. Post 44p.
ISBN 0 9527548 0 0.

A BOYHOOD PICKERING
Keith Snowden recalls living in the Twenties and Thirties, his school activities and life in wartime Pickering. This is social history in a autobiographical style.
£2.85. Post 44p. ISBN 0 9527548 2 7.

THE HOUSE OF YORK AT WAR
A Yorkist account of the Wars of the Roses.
AUTHOR'S EDITION. £2.95. Post 44p.
ISBN 0 9527548 3 5

THE ADVENTUROUS CAPTAIN COOK
The life and voyages of James Cook, R.N.,F.R.S.
Here is the life of this great Yorkshire-born navigator and his exciting voyages of discovery.
£2.99. Post 44p. ISBN 0 9527548 4 3.

ON SALE IN LOCAL BOOKSHOPS, OR DIRECT FROM THE PUBLISHER : CASTLEDEN PUBLICATIONS,
11 Castlegate, Pickering, North Yorkshire, YO18 7AX.
Telephone 01751 476227.
Post free on five or more copies.